GAME-CHANGING QUARTERBACKS

JAYDEN DANIELS

Gareth Stevens PUBLISHING

BY P. J. FREEDMAN

HOT TOPICS

Please visit our website, www.garethstevens.com. For a free color catalog of all our high-quality books, call toll free 1-800-542-2595 or fax 1-877-542-2596.

Library of Congress Cataloging-in-Publication Data
Names: Freedman, P. J., author.
Title: Jayden Daniels / P. J. Freedman.
Description: Buffalo, New York : Gareth Stevens Publishing, 2026. | Series: Game-changing quarterbacks | Includes index.
Identifiers: LCCN 2024053455 (print) | LCCN 2024053456 (ebook) | ISBN 9781482472479 (library binding) | ISBN 9781482472462 (paperback) | ISBN 9781482472486 (ebook)
Subjects: LCSH: Daniels, Jayden, 2000- | Football players–United States–Biography–Juvenile literature. | Quarterbacks (Football)–United States–Biography–Juvenile literature. | Washington Commanders–Juvenile literature.
Classification: LCC GV939.D335 F744 2026 (print) | LCC GV939.D335 (ebook) | DDC 796.332092 [B]–dc23/eng/20250116
LC record available at https://lccn.loc.gov/2024053455
LC ebook record available at https://lccn.loc.gov/2024053456

Published in 2026 by
Gareth Stevens Publishing
2544 Clinton Street
Buffalo, NY 14224

Cover Designer: Nicholas Switalski
Interior Designer: Rachel Rising
Editor: Kristen Nelson

Photo credits: Cover, pp. 1, 23, 27 UPI / Alamy Stock Photo; Back Cover, EFKS/Shutterstock.com; pp. 3-32 swissdrone/Shutterstock.com; pp. 3, 4, 6, 8, 10, 12, 14,16, 18, 20, 22, 24, 26, 28, 30, 31, 32 Logvin art/Shutterstock.com; pp. 3, 4, 5, 6, 8, 12, 18, 20, 24, 26, 30, 31, 32 Dadan Andriyana/ Shutterstock.com; pp. 4, 6, 9, 10, 13, 15, 16, 18, 21, 23, 25, 27, 28, 30 MamasOmar/ Shutterstock.com; p. 5 eksandr Poliashenko/Shutterstock.com; pp. 5, 10, 14, 16, 22, 28 Kovalov Anatolii/Shutterstock.com; p. 5 ZUMA Press, Inc. / Alamy Stock Photo; pp. 7, 25 Kirby Lee / Alamy Stock Photo; pp. 9, 11, 13, 15, 17, 19, 21 Cal Sport Media / Alamy Stock Photo; p. 29 AFF / Alamy Stock Photo.

Printed in the United States of America

CPSIA compliance information: Batch #CSGS26: For further information contact Gareth Stevens, at 1-800-542-2595.

CONTENTS

FUTURE GOAT?

Jayden Daniels hasn't been in the National Football League (NFL) for long, but he's already making his mark. He's known in the locker room for his hard work. He's known in the league for being able to throw the ball deep, even while on the run.

IN THE POCKET

DANIELS STARTED USING A VIRTUAL REALITY HEADSET AS PART OF HIS TRAINING IN COLLEGE. HE STILL USES IT IN THE NFL!

COMMANDERS

MEET THE FAMILY

Daniels was born on December 18, 2000, in San Bernardino, California. His mom, Regina Jackson, and his dad, Javon Daniels, met in high school. Daniels has a sister too.

IN THE POCKET

DANIELS WAS VERY CLOSE TO HIS GRANDPA. HIS GRANDPA TOOK HIM TO FOOTBALL PRACTICE WHEN HE WAS YOUNGER.

REGINA JACKSON

QB HOPEFUL

Daniels's dad played cornerback at the University of Washington. He passed on his love of football to his son. At first, Daniels played many positions. But he truly wanted to have the ball in his hands. He wanted to be a quarterback!

IN THE POCKET

DANIELS PICTURED HIMSELF PLAYING IN THE NFL WHEN HE WAS JUST 12 YEARS OLD.

Daniels started working with a trainer. His dad helped him too. He put in a lot of work to learn what it takes to play quarterback. It paid off! Daniels played quarterback for four years for the Cajon High School Cowboys.

IN THE POCKET

DANIELS STARTED RUNNING TRACK AT AGE 7. HE RAN SPRINT EVENTS AS WELL AS THE LONGER 400-METER.

RISE UP
CAJON
5

HIGH SCHOOL STANDOUT

Daniels was a superstar at Cajon High School. He led the team to a championship in 2017! By Daniels's last year in high school, Cajon football games were selling out. Daniels began to be **recruited** by college football programs.

IN THE POCKET

IN JANUARY 2024, CAJON HIGH SCHOOL CHANGED THE NAME OF ITS FOOTBALL STADIUM TO JAYDEN DANIELS STADIUM.

ASU SUCCESS

Daniels started playing for the Arizona State University (ASU) Sun Devils in 2019. He started 12 games as a freshman, or first year, player. By the end of the season, he had thrown for 2,943 yards and 17 touchdowns. He only threw two **interceptions** all season!

IN THE POCKET

DANIELS WAS NAMED THE MVP OF THE SUN BOWL ON DECEMBER 31, 2019!

The COVID-19 **pandemic** shortened the 2020 football season. Still, Daniels started the four games ASU played. He started every game in 2021 too. He led the Sun Devils to eight wins, throwing 2,381 yards in total.

IN THE POCKET

DANIELS LED THE PAC-12 IN COMPLETION PERCENTAGE IN 2021. THE PAC-12 IS A CONFERENCE, OR GROUPING OF TEAMS THAT PLAY EACH OTHER, MOSTLY IN THE WESTERN PART OF THE UNITED STATES.

PT-42
ASU
5
SUN DEVILS

MOVING ON

Daniels made a hard decision in 2022. He left ASU. Daniels left partly because he wanted to be part of a bigger football program. He chose Louisiana State University (LSU). The coaches there made him feel like they really wanted him!

IN THE POCKET

WHILE AT LSU, DANIELS MADE DEALS WITH BEATS BY DRE, POWERADE, AND OTHER COMPANIES. HE MADE A LOT OF MONEY FROM THESE DEALS!

#RECORD-BREAKING

Daniels became the starting quarterback for the LSU Tigers. He led the team to the Southeastern Conference (SEC) championship game, though they lost to the University of Georgia. In the 2022 season, Daniels broke the school record for rushing touchdowns by a quarterback with 11.

IN THE POCKET

DANIELS ALSO SET AN LSU RECORD FOR MOST RUSHING YARDS BY A QUARTERBACK WITH 885.

In Daniels's last year playing college football, he led the Tigers to 10 regular season wins. He ended with a record-setting career total of 12,000 passing yards and 3,000 rushing yards. Daniels won the 2023 Heisman Trophy, or prize, for best college football player that year!

IN THE POCKET

SPORTS SEASONS WERE SHORTENED OR CANCELLED DURING THE COVID-19 PANDEMIC. BECAUSE OF THIS, DANIELS AND OTHERS WHO PLAYED COLLEGE SPORTS WERE ALLOWED TO PLAY AN EXTRA YEAR IF THEY CHOSE TO. DANIELS DID!

GETTING DRAFTED

The Washington Commanders picked Daniels in the 2024 NFL **Draft**. He was chosen second overall. At the time, the Commanders had three other quarterbacks on the team. Daniels knew he had to work hard to earn the starting position.

IN THE POCKET

ONE OF THE COMMANDERS' COACHES SAID OF DANIELS AFTER HE STARTED WORKING WITH THE TEAM: "IT'S NOT ANY MAGIC THAT'S GOING INTO THIS... HE REALLY PUTS IN THE WORK."

COMMANDER ON THE FIELD

Daniels was named starting quarterback for the Commanders and had a great first NFL season. After nine games, he only had two interceptions! Daniels led the team to a winning season with 12 wins and only five losses.

IN THE POCKET

THE SPOTLIGHT SHONE ON DANIELS IN OCTOBER 2024 WHEN HE THREW A HAIL MARY PASS 52 YARDS DOWN THE FIELD TO SCORE—AND WIN THE GAME!

Daniels is one of the best young players in the NFL! His hard work and talent were recognized in 2025 when he was named NFL Offensive Rookie of the Year! What will he accomplish next?

IN THE POCKET

DANIELS WAS PART OF A SHOW ABOUT COLLEGE ATHLETES CALLED *THE MONEY GAME* THAT CAME OUT IN 2024.

JAYDEN DANIELS'S FOOTBALL TIMELINE

2017	Daniels wins a championship with the Cajon High School Cowboys.
2019	Daniels starts playing football at Arizona State University.
2022	He changes schools to Louisiana State University. He plays for the Tigers as the starting quarterback.
2023	He wins the Heisman Trophy.
2024	Daniels is chosen by the Washington Commanders in the NFL Draft.
2025	He is named NFL Offensive Rookie of the Year.

FOR MORE INFORMATION

BOOKS

Klepeis, Alicia. *The Washington Commanders.* Minneapolis, MN: Bellwether Media, 2024.

Roland, James. *The Next Generation: NFL Star Quarterbacks.* San Diego, CA: ReferencePoint Press, 2025.

WEBSITES

Jayden Daniels
https://www.commanders.com/team/players-roster/jayden-daniels/
Follow Daniels's career with the Commanders here.

Jayden Daniels
https://lsusports.net/sports/fb/roster/player/jayden-daniels/
Check out Daniels's college stats!

Publisher's note to educators and parents: Our editors have carefully reviewed these websites to ensure that they are suitable for students. Many websites change frequently, however, and we cannot guarantee that a site's future contents will continue to meet our high standards of quality and educational value. Be advised that students should be closely supervised whenever they access the internet.

GLOSSARY

completion percentage: The number of successful passes thrown by a quarterback divided by the number of total throws. This is multiplied by 100 to make a percentage.

draft: The process of selecting new players for a league.

interception: When a quarterback's pass is caught by the opposing team.

MVP: Most valuable, or best, player.

pandemic: A time when a disease, or sickness, spreads quickly and affects a large number of people in a place or throughout the world.

recruit: To try to bring an athlete to a team.

sprint: To run as fast as possible for a short distance.

stadium: A large building where sporting events take place.

virtual reality: Having to do with technology that is used to make a pretend world that can be seen using special tools, such as a headset or glasses.

INDEX